RACING SPORTS

# KART RACING

BY MARY MAXWELL

WWW.APEXEDITIONS.COM



Apex is distributed by North Star Editions:
sales@northstareditions.com | 888-417-0195

Produced for Apex by Red Line Editorial.

Photographs ©: Shutterstock Images, cover, 1, 4–5, 6–7, 8–9, 10–11, 14, 15, 16–17, 18–19, 26, 29; AP Images, 12; Fritz Polt/Times-Republican/AP Images, 13; Wikimedia Commons, 20–21; iStockphoto, 22–23, 24–25, 27

**Library of Congress Control Number: 2022923640**

**ISBN**
978-1-63738-538-8 (hardcover)
978-1-63738-592-0 (paperback)
978-1-63738-698-9 (ebook pdf)
978-1-63738-646-0 (hosted ebook)

Printed in the United States of America
Mankato, MN
082023

## NOTE TO PARENTS AND EDUCATORS

**Apex books are designed to build literacy skills in striving readers. Exciting, high-interest content attracts and holds readers' attention. The text is carefully leveled to allow students to achieve success quickly. Additional features, such as bolded glossary words for difficult terms, help build comprehension.**

# TABLE OF CONTENTS

CHAPTER 1

# READY TO RACE

It is race day. Crews check the karts. Drivers put on their helmets. They line up the karts at the starting grid.

The starting grid spaces out the drivers before the race begins.

The race starts, and the karts take off. The drivers zoom down the track. They swerve around corners and speed down **straightaways**.

**FAST FACT**

Turning can slow drivers down. So, drivers try to move in straight lines.

Drivers try to gain speed on the straightaways.

A kart's tires grip the track to keep it from skidding or flipping over.

The karts all race toward the finish line. One driver zips past the others. He crosses the finish line and wins the race.

## WARMING UP

**Before races, drivers do practice laps. This driving warms up their karts' tires. Warm tires grip the racetrack better. The karts can go faster and avoid crashing.**

# CHAPTER 2

# KART RACING HISTORY

Kart racing started in the United States in the 1950s. Some people didn't need the engines from their old lawn mowers. They used the engines to make small **vehicles**.

Many lawn mowers use small engines to spin blades that cut grass.

**Some groups organized kart races for kids. Others held races for adults.**

Soon, kart racing spread across the United States and Europe. Many groups formed to **organize** rules and races. The first racetrack just for karts was built in 1958.

## QUEEN OF KART RACING

Faye Pierson was an early kart-racing star. She was nicknamed Ladybug. She raced in important events around the world. In 1959, she came in second in the US national championship.

Kart races aren't usually divided by gender.

Kart racing is popular in countries all over the world.

In 2022, drivers from more than 50 countries did **competitive** races. Many people also race karts just for fun.

## FAST FACT

**Many young drivers start out as kart racers before moving on to other racing styles.**

Jeff Gordon is best known for winning NASCAR races. But he started out racing karts.

CHAPTER 3

# HOW IT WORKS

There are three main types of kart racing. The most common is sprint racing. Drivers race on small courses with left and right turns.

Sprint tracks can be up to 1 mile (1.6 km) long.

Other kart races happen on speedways. These tracks are shaped like ovals. They have straightaways and only left turns.

FAST FACT

Some speedways are paved. Others are made of dirt, clay, or sand.

In speedway races, drivers make 4 to 20 laps around the track.

In enduro karts, drivers lean back and are low to the ground. This helps the karts move faster.

Enduro races are longer. Races can last an hour or more. Drivers race along real roads. And they use a different style of karts. Instead of sitting up as they drive, the drivers **recline**.

## RACING ROUNDS

Most kart races have several rounds called heats. The fastest drivers from early rounds move on. The final round determines the race's winner.

CHAPTER 4

# EQUIPMENT

Karts are **open-wheel** vehicles. They are made from steel and have strong engines. The fastest karts can reach 150 miles per hour (241 km/h).

Karts usually weigh around 165 pounds (75 kg).

For racing, karts are divided into groups called classes. Karts of similar size and power race against one another. Drivers are grouped by age or **experience**.

Younger racers often use karts with smaller engines.

FAST FACT

Kids as young as five can compete in kart races.

Kart racing can be dangerous. Drivers could break bones or get **whiplash**. So, drivers wear helmets. Some wear neck braces, too. This helps them stay safe.

Many racers wear gloves to protect their hands.

## SAFETY FLAGS

If there is a crash or problem, people at the racetrack wave flags. The flags warn the drivers to stop or slow down. Each color sends a different message.

A yellow flag tells drivers to be careful, go slow, and not pass other karts.

# COMPREHENSION QUESTIONS

*Write your answers on a separate piece of paper.*

1. Write a few sentences that explain the main ideas of Chapter 3.
2. Would you want to try kart racing? Why or why not?
3. What type of kart racing uses oval racetracks?
    - **A.** sprint
    - **B.** speedway
    - **C.** enduro
4. Why might drivers start racing karts before switching to other racing styles?
    - **A.** Kids can start kart racing at a young age.
    - **B.** Karts are bigger and faster than most race cars.
    - **C.** Drivers cannot compete in kart racing.

**5.** What does **courses** mean in this book?

*Drivers race on small **courses** with left and right turns.*

- **A.** tracks for racing
- **B.** kinds of karts
- **C.** straight lines

**6.** What does **determines** mean in this book?

*The fastest drivers from early rounds move on. The final round **determines** the race's winner.*

- **A.** loses
- **B.** decides
- **C.** stops

*Answer key on page 32.*

# GLOSSARY

**competitive**

Taking part in events where people try to win games or sports.

**experience**

The amount of time people have spent doing or practicing something.

**open-wheel**

Having wheels on the outside of the car.

**organize**

To arrange and plan.

**recline**

To lie back.

**straightaways**

The parts of racetracks that are straight.

**vehicles**

Things like ships, cars, and trains that people can ride in.

**whiplash**

An injury that happens when someone's head is jerked back and forth, such as in a car crash.

# TO LEARN MORE

## BOOKS

Adamson, Thomas K. *Karts*. Minneapolis: Bellwether Media, 2019.

Amstutz, Lisa J. *The Gearhead's Guide to Go-Karts*. North Mankato, MN: Capstone Press, 2023.

Shaffer, Lindsay. *ATVs*. Minneapolis: Bellwether Media, 2019.

## ONLINE RESOURCES

Visit **www.apexeditions.com** to find links and resources related to this title.

## ABOUT THE AUTHOR

Mary Maxwell is an author and playwright. When she races, she prefers to be on a bicycle.

# INDEX



**ANSWER KEY:**
1. Answers will vary; 2. Answers will vary; 3. B; 4. A; 5. A; 6. B